Put On The Noise

Marion J. Goff
Alexandra L. Karambelas
Devin K. Karambelas

First Light Over Second Beach
October 30th 2019
—mg

ISBN: 978-0-578-92203-4

Copyright © 2021 Marion J. Goff
Cover design & layout © 2021 Joanne Birdsell

All rights reserved. No part of this book may be used or reproduced in any manner without written permission from the author except in the case of reprints in the context of reviews.

For Dennis,
  For Dad,
    Our Head Heart & Soul
  Dr. Dennis Karambelas

On October 1st 2017 my sweet sweet husband of almost thirty years, Dr. Dennis Karambelas, who was a prominent optometrist in Providence, RI, died from cancer only three months following diagnosis. He was a very youthful 65 year old who was adored by most everyone who knew him, a Capricorn born on the Epiphany of January 6th, as he liked to tell everyone. He was an exceptional fun loving father to our twin daughters, Alexandra and Devin, and he was an amazing husband, soul mate, business partner, optometrist, son, brother and friend, basketball player, and chess coach to our girls and their classmates.

When Dennis passed away the world lost one of the good ones, one of the great ones. Always a believer in educating oneself, Dennis was at the top of his profession as a Fellow and Diplomate of the American Academy of Optometry in Cornea and Contact Lenses. He generously shared his knowledge and expertise with other doctors over his career. He made sure he found the best science, the best contact lens worldwide so that his thousands of patients could see and would be happy with their vision, many of whom had severe vision loss due to disease or injury. You could say he was a visionary!

He attended the University of Pennsylvania as an undergraduate on a chess scholarship and would forevermore be a loyal Penn grad, loving the school and the Palestra, as Dennis was a huge basketball fan for the Penn women's and men's basketball teams and for his own Boston Celtics. When we lost Dennis who was Dad to our girls, we lost the center of our lives. This poetry book comes from our deep love and loss as a tribute to this wonderful man who made our lives and the lives of so many, so much better. He is so deeply missed. This book, this gift is created with love from everyone he touched.

"Courage doesn't always roar. Sometimes courage is the quiet voice at the end of the day saying, 'I will try again tomorrow'."

Mary Anne Radmacher

We thank Joanne Birdsell for creating a cover that reflects the poetry we have dedicated to someone who was the center of our lives, Dennis Karambelas. Her art represents the sound, the voice and the essence of family before and after it experiences loss.

Thank You Tom F. Bohan & The Georgia Bohans!

Thank You Ingrid Bennett .. A Capricorn Heaven Sent, whose light helps us find our Spirit again.

Our Deepest Gratitude to Donna Garcia & Scott Albert.

Very Special Thanks!
Joanne Birdsell
Marilyn "Mel" Roberti
Hannah J. Oliver

With Thanks to Our Angels!
Dr. Robert Child
Renee Buisson & Dave Betsch
Sharon & Paul Caine
Tom & Carol Goff
June Patricia Goff Dearborn
Carol & Tom Bohan
Lois Karambelas & Jim McCarthy
Stu & Amy Dorosko Moran
Cara Lynn O'Shea
Father Stephen Amaral

Charles Karambelas, Byron & David Rizos
Andy Blidy
Deb Pires
Joan Collins
Robin Kent
Maggie Ross
Bernadette Ottiano
Patricia White Delfino
Kathleen Kelly & John Sullivan
Joanne Hayes & John Nicolace
Judy & Frank Russell
Rob & Jess Mencunas
Chris M. Bohan
Jason M. & Sonia Rodriguez Bohan
Brent & Melissa Bohan Hallenbeck
Chris & Jaclyn Rose Caine
Rob Dearborn & Victoria Albert
Victoria & Sarah Goff
Josie K. Dearborn
Dave & Tina Dearborn
Jim Bowker
Barney Zimmermann
Ron Carmark
Channa Lincoln
Derek Braslow
Jennifer Gehringer Puerini
Gil Bianchi
Sarah Isherwood

Table Of Contents

Part I Loss

1	Living room furniture
2	A thousand nights
3	Put on the Noise
6	Red Barn
7	The Thing That Rots
9	Strange Tide
10	Sunday Yoga
11	You can't be lost in a nameless place
13	Outline
15	Prayer
17	Light Part I
19	Light Part II
21	please describe the pain (parts 1&2)
23	What is the sound we make?
25	August
26	TS
27	And on and on the record sang
28	for devin & alex october 31st 3am
29	You can try to be better
30	Talking to Michael
31	You were cool
32	Adirondack Chairs
33	Poem To Denís
34	angels really
35	Why do human beings break
36	mostly maskless
37	Driving directionless
38	Writing in the rain
39	Newton Nap
40	Just shy of al dente
41	We write our own narrative
42	poem to my daughters

43	The cardinal calls
44	sundown
45	Daisy
46	Hungarian Pastry Shop
49	Lunch in Liechtenstein
51	Rooks & Pawns
52	for ray walker
53	Selina
54	Season Sanity
55	This is what I can no longer do..

Part II Leap

59	healer
61	bicker
62	circadian clock
63	Bookends
66	tiptoe
67	egret haiku
68	Egret
69	Comeback
70	For me
71	Today I felt like shining
72	March Winds
73	fifty years
74	Cardinal calls winter
75	egret haiku prayer
76	warrior
77	high
78	white and weathered
79	As if.. For Kim & Victoria
81	Three Julys
82	You are never going to be ready
83	Chiron
85	Somewhere in the spring of my life

Part I
Loss

Living room furniture

A chair falls apart
Leather isn't meant to last
I sink, remember

We tried rearranging
Once. And moved it by the
window
(we tried many things)
(then we un-tried them)

Morning light finds my
legs sideways over warped arm
Highball suspended

How did it find yours?

Chairs fall apart but
it belonged to someone I
Remember. I sink

      —dk

A thousand nights

And I will lay alone a night
a thousand nights it's been
And I will seek an answer to
one thousand and one questions
Of how the strongest bonds
of love of family most special
could fall apart
for in the end
we really are all just fragile
—mg

Put on the Noise

My mother decided to take my father's
Appointment, at the holistic doctors office

Five days after he died. It was hard to get
In to see him- months even, and my

Father's disease still hung around the air
Like we could catch it, and without life

Insurance until the 30th
She was worried about things like "what if I died

Too?" Imagine- a time where she had the
Luxury to worry about her own flesh.

Not the way we imagined it.

When she wasn't trying to squeeze
Someone's palm hard enough to wring out

The pain they had inside them,
As if it could be transferred, rug to hand, the shock

Like flint to rock, when two things cannot
Be at once and so they fight for space

Sending up big fiery sparks
Like how you can be everywhere-

Your coffee cup, your rain jacket
Yet nowhere to be found.

"This is great that you're doing this"
I told her. She grimaced, sucked in her
Cheeks and turned her mouth upwards
In a breathless gauze covered smile.

They will see her, and help her, I thought.
The old trick. We could push our sadness all

The way out to the limit until they get swept
In by savior, white light, white coat.

Let them take care of this. Let them figure this out
Like I could pawn off my fear and sell it

To Blue Cross, to the hospital that wouldn't waive the 5
Dollar parking garage charge when I couldn't pay

It. So they pointed me the way to the bus-
You cost too much. Let somebody else take this.

Had we given my father away like that? I didn't think much
Of humanity when I walked away from the lot that night.

The kids don't talk back anymore. The
Best I can do is make the house warm

For her when she comes home. Put on the
Noise, the chatter of wine glasses against

The counter. These are the sounds I would like to
Remember like laughter and stomping

Off shoes when we came in. My sister animated in a story
The sound of the leather chair stretching as he would lean
Forward to hear what she was saying.
Put on the TV, the radio,
My shoes are louder now and stand on heels that
Talk
Across
Floors

Anything to make me move faster from the quiet
That makes us hear something cracking inside us
Like the sound that kindness makes when it gives you a

Small space to rest in

—ak

Red Barn

You held my hand when we rounded the corners, lazy hills
All wrapped up and kept close
As the white snow that tucked the trees in a long blanket
-A little red barn stood weathered and proud like a heart place.
Out here, away from town
The sky is always big
And swallows the ground until a mountain is a cloud
(And I don't even need to tell you about heaven)
Where everything is whitewashed
And your face is crinkled around the bright spot in your eyes
That catches light like it's splashing up water.

I've fallen in enough times to know my heart
   sags
      like an old barn
It creaks in the wind and feels things it never did before
When the foundations were put up with a whole lot of work and
a little bit of joy
To be able to build
Now it knows that in order to stand
It must bend
And move with the weather that beats upon it every day
Here, where all the people have left
It lays all
  the way
    back
      into its scenery
Undoes a latch, lets its screen door blow back and forth
It opens itself up
To the snowstorms that break in a window
Lets its wood scratch through the paint
Until it cracks and again betrays
 Itself
Exposed endlessly
—It fits right into nature, knows it is home
Tucked in, there is something warm
And as easy as a hand
fitting into another

                        —ak

The Thing That Rots

I read somewhere that the west doesn't touch enough dead bodies-
That we fear our own dust because we are able to
Discard the thing that rots

We close the lid
Have a whole continent to bury them
Under.

We are allowed to pull the curtain, look away
From the television.

When we sit with sickness it looks across the room at us,
 As someone separate
The rot is outside the window, despite a feeling
That sits and festers in our stomachs

And when we eat, we hold our prey below us
In nails that scalpel-glint
And smell of the sterilization of life.

I could have read this in a library in a house
 That smells of old books and wealth
Where I can see a man sitting in a leather chair
A different kind of dust flies into the air at the touch
 And gives its particular aura of treasure
  Of relic, of a succession of men absentmindedly spinning the globe

The longing for distant places, old heroes
Leaves us picking apart the ground for our own bones
Like if we look long enough into the past
We will find ourselves
    Stuck in the middle of a hieroglyphic map

Whose copy, dated and weathered hangs above
The chair
With legs carved into talons
That grip the ball of the earth
In refined, thick chokehold
-It is hard to remember where we have been
When we rarely touch the place we all are going.

When soft creatures move out from semi darkness
They pull stiffness out of their flesh
Grow horns, become prickly
Calcified
Some kind of strange evolution
With all the water gone
We have learned to grow claws, snakeskin thick like leather
There are only so many ways to survive in a landscape so arid
You've got to hold what you used to swim in
Inside of you, in hollowed caves

-I wonder if I too will grow scales
Harden up
Crystalize what used to dew, and drop
Scrape myself until I become the kind
Of jagged that can scratch and bite back
Does evolution work that fast?

So,

Who is farthest from the thing that rots?
Is it us? Have I been so far in proximity
To those things that are diseased
That my immunity is
Shot? I don't have venom
 In my teeth, or skin that's hard like rock
How are we to live down there?
And where exactly and who sits in the chair
While we all scramble just to eat
                              —ak

Strange Tides

We take fresh water whole, into our mouth
And turn it into oceans in our eyes
In so many ways we are brackish
We learn to live in two worlds
Listen and look at each other when we are speaking
Sometimes
I feel a camera zoom and click
Mindlessly interrupt the flow
Startle myself with the flash
The quakes of when I've looked at this as it's come to pass
I remember, I remember, I swim in it
It fills my eyes and soon my lungs are
Full and brimming

I feel it here, everywhere
The stillness
That whispers
"Pay attention"
Is this why everything is muted
Why the light comes through filtered and the sound says nothing?
Have I reached the place where I feel my years when they will come
-and they will come
Over every inch of this
When it's gone?
This, my whole life, a rainstorm
Dripping into itself

These are strange tides that pull me back and forth.
My throat has been gone for weeks and the act of speaking is exhausting
All I can do is listen to them
Mouth something like remember.
Waves always try to claw their way to land
Taking this too, and this too
What more do you want, isn't the ocean enough?
But they still come over what they can that's dry and breathing
—ak

Sunday Yoga

I laid on the carpet, unfurled in the same vegetal growth
As its Persian design and muted colors that keep
The room still.
I hug the ground with my chest open, and fall deep into
something old as
Shale deposits- socketed, cool and clothesline damp
Held tight by starchy threads
It is throbbing, to drag my world back into one small note
Of single cell organisms- before something inside, or outside of
us quaked with movement
When the root of us tethered and flapped in the current of a
deep erosion
We broke
Apart in fragmentation, multiplying voices
Duplicating notes, all in the motion of harmonies and
disharmonies.
To hear them all at once, as we do today
Is a deafening thing.
Once more we flee to the water to bury our head
To remember when we first learned to walk
-I find I can't sink into that stillness
My flesh is immovable, it speaks in the deep pockets of my
hips something of resistance
It wants to take me somewhere above that ground,
Away from a core that's saturated with blood and fire.
It only knows how to freeze, not to dig into what my animal
eyes cannot see

—ak

You can't be lost in a nameless place

Here,
Where white sand is a few shades paler than dust
We fell to our knees, one leg at a time
And squinted into the sun. Our clothes had dirt in the creases
 were ragged, lips
Chapped and parched
Our foreheads slick and shining like a fresh oil leak from a truck off the highway
-We must have looked crazy as we tried to conjure up a mirage

It was hard to imagine that talons
Could stretch out and snatch us out here
There were no signs
Or street corners
Or people
Or names
In a place where a sand storm could arch its back
Make its ears stand, prickle its hairs
Whisper things
Before it began
Before it gave us fury
Until we couldn't see our hands.

Every inch of this land was silent
Held by the full drone of wind that lashed about in any
Direction, absurd
And so said nothing, and left us
with our own
Thoughts, of the places we had left
Behind squeezed into the hallway
closet with linens from our loved ones
  We kissed it all goodnight and fled to a place that was faceless
Where the sky and ground and our lives blended

To a point
Of complete
  Still-
The desert is full of footprints
Car tracks that lead you to the mountains
The creatures here have eyes so black that mercy never did fall off their tongues
With quite as much ease as their skin
Shedding layers snakelike
Leaving them scattered like corpses
To burn under the sun
Like everything else.

You coil back in fear and turn to me
Uncertain I am not something here to lead you astray
Take you to the edge where you will never be seen again
Until I too shed you
It's no wonder people out here can't stop running
In a place so still
You could see your thoughts
Before you like a grand and sacred omen
It's so easy to look away
To run from oasis to oasis to search
For new waters from well to well

                              —ak

Outline

I've been trying to measure the way he moved through time
    In those last months
Tried to remember our last glass of wine together
The last time he cracked a joke, our last vacation
The last time he smiled or rolled his eyes
Any kind of clue as to where I could find him
    Places where I should have paid attention
To the parts of himself we somehow planted
Like we ran away in the middle of the night, in a thunderstorm,
And buried it
Where nobody, not even us, could find it.
It's hard to tell
When we're always moving too.

Today I cried happy tears
Kept the little drops of water balanced in my hands on my fingers
Like they were holy water, miracle miracle
-who knows how long they've been there.
When looking at a descending plane make a bright last streak across the sky
Staring hard and close from down here, we cannot see it move even one inch
For that we have to look away
See the trace lines
Understand it's always in passing.

I would be lying if I didn't tell you
It's been hard lately
to talk about an ache
Without being vague
There are just too many
Places it can hurt at once.
Describe it, go ahead and try
It will move through you faster than you can realize it's

Always leaving
There are so many places it touches I almost believe our eyes
created horizons as if to raise a hand and say:
Enough.

I thank the nature around us for her boundaries, her outlines
That the seasons let us touch the passage of time
My own seasons too, roll in like weather, hang around in dark forest walls.
Look closely, see that they become tiny, to be held in the hand
When we measure small
moments-
Like landmarks.
Mine to keep, and change.

Today I felt the fault lines quake from a place that
Breaks inside me like ice
Wondered, am I of two pieces? Split -me
Before this, the me that's after.
Or is it like a plane slicing a mark in the sky
Putting two sides and a dividing line across
Blue, whole and full
I can't help but feel it's as putting a lid over the air and naming it separate
Or trying to fit the stratosphere into a rectangle, print and keep it.
My tears come from the same well
You when you threw me over your shoulder when I was a kid
You when they drained light from your eyes
I cry for both
I cannot make lines for long
They blend into the sky and soon the plane has landed, its clues vanished.
But I suppose the only thing we have in this far too big world
Are our own tracings, and our own names
It's the way you and I can change the way we're made
To have the last word.

         —ak

Prayer

There was discomfort when I developed growth lines on my thighs
I look at them often, despite the many years of topical creams meant to erase
the places where my body had thought it was done
and then, was stretched past that reasoning.
I noticed them while I was sitting cross-legged in high school, and then at my first desk job
Straddling two worlds- one of which I was, and one which I would be
For now, I am still mid-jump over a drop that shows me I am nowhere- mid flight and blurred unrecognizable.
I think I like that best. I had always felt more like myself while traveling,
Constantly in motion and reading my story aloud like I was fiction.
I am repeating the message so that each cell hears and acts accordingly- we are not pain, despite the fact that when I see beauty and name it, I too become beautiful.
It's been a hard few years, no doubt about it.
I love you, I love you I repeat
Often enough to lose and find its sacredness
I've been understanding prayer despite methodical sarcasm
I've been understanding prayer as (I love you, I love you.)
Some days a song comes on and I'm all awash in a tiny moment, that I had held and did not know had been saved.
Startling- I would like to control them like I was harnessing their wild and unpredictable energy
I would like to think of you in all fruit and flowers, that much I know.
Talking is too hard, when everything is sacred.
I've been walking around conversation like I was hopping over a long graveyard
Careful not to step on the grass where your memory
Lies below it

But to shed this is not to leave you, I think
Grief is heavy, it pulls you towards the dirt
I will lower that burden all the way down low until something has got to break
And fall to kiss my feet
Like leaves hugging the base of a tree
You will be back in some other, yet another form
(there are so many ways in which the bloom is eternal)
Picking up the old stitch
Season after seasonal sameness
Not the singular petals or the flower but the whole field
Is alive,
Comes back year after year
There is some kind of a blessing in the thought that we must change to come home
That your memory- alive without the singular you
Still breathes your life, still speaks for you

           —ak

Light Part I

"Patience is perfect" something says, and almost wakes me
We are lying in the halfway place
Still as midnight down an empty side street
Where street lamps glow like fluorescent orbs and create a fuzzy halo that blends the light and night
You stir all wrapped in a dream that leaks out of your breath
And for a minute I realize that I am happy.

What a blessing it is to trust the place
we live in again
Feel water stream through old pathways, see dust turn
Into mineral life
That pools its way through old halls, old hard rock bed
Spaces where the weight wanted me to meet
the dirt I'm going to lay under
I've looked enough times to know how memory leaves one hand empty, the other holding the heart
Until she comes to take the longest part of you too
Better leave it to shadow, bury it in the long pause before their name
nobody could ever understand how deep this runs
even we can't hope to see the bottom.

I take myself back up to the surface where I can see the sun
Pull off the covers in the morning, pick colors
Listen close- there is something begging to see daylight through me
It bubbles up until my eyes and mouth become a spring
And then light begets light and I'm blinking, catching and throwing some kind of vividness

I declare this place happiness

Not the kind that excites, flutters and leaves
No, this is slow and deep
Watch me plant each foot down in its earth like I was erecting a flag
It is a choice I make every day that I get out of bed
Let the sun kiss my skin, touch the world back with movement

I'll speak it until a cooler night comes and my breath draws ice and exhales
some kind of smoke from the light we carry inside
We will look at the stars until they seem to stare back into our own eyes
And we can lift ourselves up from where we will be laying
In the hopes of reflecting light
blinking
falling
dancing
across the sky kind of light

—ak

Light Part II

I'm sprawled out onto you in the kind of early morning limpness
Flowers in the backyard get in wind-rain
When everything is bowing under the water and the wetness
Brings up an earth smell
I'm somehow being held
Up by you even though we're both laying-
I think of that one rainstorm where the daffodils were pushed almost all the way to the ground, wild and horizontal.
Some mornings, you deviate from the pattern, and move another inch of my skin to touch. I am closer to feeling that every part of me has its place and belongs
In the long stretch of map that covers a body
Like this we stream through fractured places
seep through each other's cracks
Morning after
Morning light- Have you seen the way it moves
Across a field, or just our bedroom covers?
You couldn't measure it, really
And thank god minds don't calculate the space as it's being made
Just nothing— and then it's there
As if it's always been there.

I do my best to
Grow
Over myself, root and leaf
Here, twisting up— momentarily illuminated
By a patch of sun
Or maybe it is just that you are holding me
In your gaze. That's got to have some kind of subtle spotlight in the ether?

I think of the time we went walking in that patch of woods
You pulled me closer to show me
A bloom, so small
It made me bend
Down and scrunch my eyes
This had a name -it too was born when it first hit light
(And then, again,
and again). It closes and opens, practices rebirth daily.
When I got back up, I stretched my back and glanced around-
the tiny quiet molecular world, restored to scale-
For a flash, I was big again.

I suppose it's just like that: you make me feel
So large. Sometimes you make so much light it shakes me
All the way up, and my laughter could
Fill my chest, my stomach, my throat
Crinkle into my eyes
We could fill up this room
Crammed, chock full past the brim
And it still wouldn't be enough
To keep us-
We could get so big,
There could simply only be us

          —ak

please describe the pain
(parts 1&2)

eyes closed my foot feels for the flip flop
pulling woolen sweater over striped pjs
driving half awake for 6am coffee
to help steady the shock
of what remains
in our joint account
now separated
from the completeness
of what I once had with you
hello anger are you back again?
because you left so soon
so without a plan
my undying love of you
that speaks this truth of what I am without you
and the coffee burns my tongue

*

those noisy birds fell silent
as I awoke to dread
or is this emptiness
rousing me from the night before
like the jolting note struck on 3 pianos
anguish in e major
of a day in my life now
as I remember this is not a dream
so heavy I could not lift the covers
resting in this place where we find our souls
between ache and numbness
from where lightness
and laughter once breezed through
I am so out of place
I dare not go out much
to face stares from friends
now strangers

—mg

What is the sound we make
when we can no longer make sound?

you could no longer speak to me
we were not on the same wave length
silent signals in your shallow breath
searching your eyes
as you fell in and out
of consciousness
fading pulse my hand in yours
dangerous decibels
shattering
and breaking us into pieces
every part of our being
falling to the floor
tubes leads and wires
fall away
imaging kept within
of that day so many days
just fighting
to stay alive to be heard

but who will listen?
when you can't utter words

visual signals we're losing grip
touching your hand
for guidance
we were lost without language
you who could not speak
or hear
or hold a pen
searing shock screaming within
can you at least feel me?
my energy jumpstarting yours

cable to cable wire to skin
getting a message to you
give me a sign
you're still here with me

what is the sound of anguish?

the muted cacophony
of Finality
whipping around my mind
like a fierce nor'easter
violently
no visibility
bearing down exposed bent chill
hand to head
head to heart
frightened by your last gasp
your last breath
taking me in with you
then stillness

no way out
this cannot be happening
                        —mg

August

You made me fall all over myself
Like a tree when warmth allows the leaves to bloom
Something like flowers
All shook up
And growing a little too large over everything
—ak

TS

She's talking Neitzche
She's talking Derrida
I'm barely following
looking for the perfect burger

Mom you're looking for
the Transcendental
Signified
but you have the Signifier
The first was too perfect
too elusive
there will never be another

Sent me back to when we met
the Burghers 77 rue de Varenne
You my objet d'art
who I adored and admired

As we strolled Rodin's gardens
Je vous aimerai toujours
Casting dreams but never knowing
Some things already written in stone

And now I know from our young teachers
you were my Transcendental
Signified
I will never have another
You our center who gave us purpose
who gave our love form
                                         —mg

And on and on the record sang, looping back into itself where
you couldn't even tell if a track had started or ended it just
blended, into each one, into everything, it was everywhere
it played constantly, in every room, and thought, and breeze
looping around and around
in a crazy broken track of love lost and deepened
disappointment now going now stuck
playing around and around and around –broken- pausing at
those moments of sadness
and repeating them over and over again *crazily* there it is again
have we been here before
haven't I listened to this song enough am I ever going to get out
am I this song am I this song
I am this song I am this song I am this song I am this song
—ak

for devin and alex october 31st 3am

why do we forget those who die?
like I'm forgetting dad
I have forgotten dad, she said
his voice
his eyes
his kindness

and I posed this question to you
why is grief
so destructive
to be ripped apart
exposed to all?
as she carries on
her life rewritten
scripted
to compel her to join the living
who are now foreign
to us
as she tries to remember
how life once felt
laughing easily
looking forward to
all the things that form a family
a family once safe and sane

laughing eyes now sunken
voices stressed and strained

now she knows what survivors survey
in the wreck of their lives
an almost envy of those intact
unaware of the grieved
who dwell upon that of love and loss
of voice
of eyes
of memory too painful
to remember at all

—mg

You can try to be better

I can see the stretch lines on your kindness and realize you are
pulling yourself farther than you have before
But once I let go, once you let go, once anything gives way to
the weight
It will snap back a thousand miles and leave you wrinkled and
small
Where I left you
Worse, than I left you
I too have had my kindness stretched and it has snapped back all
the way to where you find me right now
Because you let go, so I let go
The order does not matter

—ak

Talking to Michael

Talking to Michael
by the back door
I'd rather not go in anymore
Speaking with Michael
wearing his wings
roll down my window
tell him anything
He's a saint they say
as I study his face
and I wonder if I
ever held such grace

Tell me Michael
why do I always run to you
Is it because you really are
like an old lover who
would sit with me to
pour out my soul
you are an angel among angels
like one I knew long ago

Hey Michael I have to ask
why you answer my prayers
only some of the time
Michael you know
I'd like to borrow your wings
Fly to the heavens
see only beautiful things
Maybe fly to my love
he was a lot like you
but I didn't have the heart
to tell him how lost I'd be
that's why I come to you
                        —mg

You were cool

You were cooler than cool
a one of a kind beach jewel
never saw someone sparkle
like you like you
making your way into my heart
taking your place
imperceptibly
the calm I refused to see
when your kind eyes fell upon me
you're my ocean treasure
born pure pleasure
my one for the ages rock as I roll
into the essence of you
heaven sent from My Ladies who
told me to wake up
and take hold of you
change my life electrify it
Inspire me to just be and try it
lay me down in the warmth of you
ah but you were lovely you were cool
—mg

Adirondack chairs

Down by Sachuest
one in hooded down parka
one up to his knees in rough water
Is it cold outside or warmed by the sun
Am I doing okay with everything
or am I drowning?
But I can sure see that scarlet sunset
like the ones we watched
from the Adirondack chairs
Back when you were holding hands smiling next to me
before I gazed from the empty chair beside me
I felt your warm hands turn cold and wondered why
or did I tell you this but you didn't confide
..in the end we carry this with us more than our dreams
—mg

Poem to Denís

to you
I am you and we are one
the one I dream of when I rest my body down
the one who I am naked to
as I have told you all my secrets
all my pain and my pain will always exist
as it once did as it does now when I wake
and you are not here
you are not here
just the rain to return me
to the lavender fields
to the fields of grasse
of the perfumery and the green water
the bottle of wine and loaf of bread
sunbathing by cap d'antibes
running up the steps to eze
maybe we will stop to drink in the view
of a place I was never with you
the scent of lavender
je suis toi
nous sommes une

—mg

angels really

What wakes me 3am once again
mysteries of the night
who touch me to awaken senses
stir again reach for the light
pad and pen replaced by typing
on the keyboard now my confidante
whose keys I stroke without thinking
like being led on a ouija board

these words I type from deep within
some come so effortlessly
sneaking out of stolen conscious
even sleep has slipped the night
I grow so tired of one way conversation
how I long to talk to you again
someone who fit so perfectly
like a snug Isotoner glove

what clarion call makes me rise
in hopes of being with you for awhile
who calls to me in places few can hear
eager to ride this elusive lullaby
a fool's heart follows once again
somewhere between two dimensions
knowing we're parted earth and heaven
knowing it's nothing more than angels really
—mg

Why do human beings break?
Because their hearts do
What revives them back to life?
Inspiration
What creates inspiration?
So don't tell me that this does not matter
When the act of creating is a matter of survival
—ak

mostly maskless

Imagine if you died
mostly masked
imagine if you died during a pandemic
instead of three years before

And I could not see you
or be with you
holding your hand
trying to find the Penn Dartmouth
football game
on the ICU tv

for you to take your mind off
everything that night
and then I left
To go home maybe get some sleep
walk Daisy
or check in on the girls
who were just so sad about things

Talking to the nurse
about our wedding
in Mykonos
Facts she had just learned
from you
only two or three days before
you passed away

And yet I think
it could have been worse
at least I was with you
You who was
mostly maskless
rarely awake
barely breathing
not much closure
for any of us
For God's sake

     —mg

Driving directionless

Driving
directionless
In an old Volkswagen
On a rainy day

Wipers
keeping time
To the music
Of the rain swept road

Daydreams
or delusions
In these special tunes
On the Blaupunkt radio

Contemplating
words refraining
Keeping beat
To the whir of wipers

Red light
Does She See It?
Blurred before her eyes
Like so many signals
     —mg

Writing in the rain

Writing in the rain
On the street where we lost everything
By the doorway where we carved our initials
In wet cement one day

And you laughed
Said my wife the vandal
And we were not young

I am in a Volkswagen
Just like I was when I was 16
Driving
directionless
But now I am 65
The rain pulls me over
To write my pain again
To right my loss
To hear you laugh again

Where we once
carved our initials
In wet cement
By our office door

And you said
My wife the vandal
And we were not young
                    —mg

Newton Nap

She said short sleep heals
What grief sometimes steals
Under a leafy blanket of weeping beech
And magnolia's reach

She said You close your eyes
While I close mine
and we will manifest a place of happier times
Just round the sunlit corner

You close your eyes
I'll close mine For we are so tired
We just need a place to rest
Need a space to just .. be

So I'll pick you up at 5
For the long ride home
And we will not worry about anyone's feelings
But our own

Just needing a Newton nap
between the serene and unreal
We'll just leave it at that

— mg

Just shy of al dente

I was stuck to you
like pasta to a wall
like lips to a kiss
like that kid's tongue to a pole
(if you remember Christmas Story at all)

Just shy of al dente
we were underdone
soaking up the sauce and sun
Love, how is it we did not grow
old together you and me?

Just shy of al dente
You and I once the main plate
but someone screwed with our recipe
wiped you off the menu slate
Leaving me alone with the Chianti

I watch cooking shows now
Lydia Milk Street Ming
Some days I don't know
where my days end or begin
All I remember is nothing and everything
　　　　　　　　　　　　　　—mg

We write our own narrative
We do this for self
Preservation
The mind is injured
The narrative is not
meant to be read
But only to be
memorized
Maybe immortalized
                      —mg

poem to my daughters

If I someday leave you
and never get this chance
to sneak in all my wisdom
as I leave you with not much else
life is all about changing
when you think you'd rather rest
when you say I am complete
and happy
you will face another test
just take it as part of living
summon up your best defense
you will find humor in darkest spaces
when things do not make sense
try to keep yourself from falling
but when you fall feel for me
to help you up to find your balance
this is how
this is where I'll be
Keep your song playing
in your head in your heart
so you don't have to think
what becomes part of you
will get you through the worst of times
will bring you back to peace
some day back to sublime
In darkest moments you will find
my hand beside your own
and we will fly like a Chagall painting
above any stress and sadness
to the times we once knew
when the four of us flew!

—mg

the cardinal calls

the cardinal calls
sweet sounds soothe the restless night
I rise but then fall
—mg

sundown

confusion closes
the shadowy shade
of another day
when all that is forgotten
time and people slip away
and even though I try
to remember for you
life doesn't work this way
                    —mg

Daisy

you looked at me
with those sad frightened black eyes
everything about you was sad
and untrusting
good I thought
I too trust no one

*

and then we were left alone
just you and me in
a dog eat dog world
through your eyes I could see
we understood each other

*

most days you were my only reason
to get out of bed
to let you out
and let you back in
and when I awoke to the other breath in the room
it gave me comfort to know
I was not truly alone
we had changed roles
I was now the rescued one
—mg

Hungarian Pastry Shop

On Amsterdam
across from the Cathedral
of Saint John
the Divine
When Liz lived on Morningside
Before I read Joan Didion
And I was in awe
of stained glass
Rose Window facade
whose towers drew me to
this neighborhood
along Riverside

I didn't have you then
I dreamed as writers do
of creating a great story
but stories carry pain with truth
If your dad and I had met before
There's no doubt in my mind
We would have lived
around the corner of
Saint John the Divine
when I was a serious writer
when I was twenty-nine

Time passed slower then
my life did not really begin
until I met him five years after
a case of divine intervention
a belief in all things heaven sent
such are the stars
who bring souls together
strange attractors

Let's you and I reconnect
We'll meet with notebooks in hand
our poetry to share
To finish at a later time
from his worn leather chair
at the Hungarian Pastry Shop
in Morningside
on Amsterdam

We'll sit among writers
who search with their pens
between coffee stains
and poetic crumbs
that fall from verse
rewritten
That cuts through
the heaviness
of what we can't say
when we do not know
what we feel
but we try and write anyway
The whispers of words
to help us connect
what we are left with
saving our breath
that has been stolen
by the Fates of Lachesis

Trying to feel human again
when all reason is gone
facing the facade
of the Unfinished One
Maybe it's raining
maybe there's sun
in the presence of
this spiritual one
discussing Joan Didion

Who didn't speak to you
but she did speak to me
if you don't mind discussing
her year of magical thinking
and catholic with a small c
Reading a poem or two about
Joan's daughters's wedding
or your dad's passing

I'll tell you about your baptism
when you both were three
with Father Steve
in the small chapel of Matunuck
by Galilee
Holy water over your timid heads
both grandfathers happiness
but dad and I knew
you were already blessed
though unaware
of the time we had left

Nothing better than to be
with my two daughters
on a Saturday
on Amsterdam
showing each other what we wrote
sharing broken bread
the French word pain
At the Hungarian Pastry Shop
in the shadow of the Saint
Who stands magnificent
and unfinished
who calls us
from the heavens and the stars
to cherish time together
around the corner of Morningside
in this special place of ours
—mg

Lunch in Liechtenstein

We had lunch in Liechtenstein
then drove the Autobahn
in an Audi
or was it a Passat wagon?
We were running so very late
for your sister's wedding
in Vienna no less
We had decided to detour
to Hungary
to Buda and Pest
Having planned her
marriage
because
she wanted a ceremony
like ours
in Mykonos
Greece
Ours was a simple affair
just the five of us there
So beautiful the people and the harbor
the pelicans who walked with us
along the white washed
streets and houses
A fairy tale really
Then we came back to earth
had a couple of kids
Then fooled ourselves into thinking
we could do anything
As long as we had each other
that we did it together

We opened a busy
optometry practice
that took all your time
and took our life savings
It went well for a long while
to see what we had created
Two beautiful daughters who were
the center of our lives
Friends and relations
who came
to our Christmas celebrations
What would I give to have you here?
I'd give everything
but the memories that brought us here
                                        —mg

Rooks & Pawns

And so you moved one way
And so I had to move another
My heart is heavy
My eyes are droopy
My heart is full
My eyes are empty
It's not that I can't make up my mind
It's just that things change all the time
And all the time is what I have now
Without you here missing you
Days drag by like the bags under my eyes
Like my piece that doesn't know
which way to go
Like my mind doesn't know which way to turn
And my fingers that hold the same figure
That I keep there
Stuck in place
Stuck in place
One day I escaped to another life
Breezy free I felt I knew this once before
But just like the song that always takes me back
I felt the loneliness drift back in
And tuck me in for another long night
And when I awoke
My heart was crushed
My eyes were droopy
My heart was full
My eyes were open
It's not that I can't make up my mind
It's just that things change all the time
Moving back and forth
To and from you
                               —mg

for ray walker

now the wind blows things away
runs through time and carries it away
and you will come and you will go
just like the one you love
you love him so

and there's nothing anyone can say
because a wind has come and taken him away
carried him to a distant land
and you will seek what you do not understand

because there's nothing anyone can say
there's nothing left to take away
you have now seen inside your soul
and you will release what you hold

now the wind blows things away
runs through time and passes it away
and you will come and you will go
just like the one you loved
you loved him so
—mg

Selina

I often wonder where you've gone to
now that there's too much time to wonder why.
If you're still dreaming with that same wide smile
enchanting others who've gone on by

Yes I wonder if you hear me nights
when my thoughts pour out to you
telling you I'm worried about the family
asking what it is you think I should do

I've tried forgetting
It hurts remembering
But there's just no ending my thoughts of you, Selina

You were June's child, spring and summer
our lively breath of autumn magic
But when winter took you all for its own
our young seasons turned tragic

So I wonder why I feel out of place so often
why the laughter inside me just disappears
I ask night after night as you're looking over
What was the secret we had all those years?

I've tried forgetting
It hurts remembering
But there's just no ending my thoughts of you
Selina, my friend

—mg

Season Sanity

Seclusion
Window shakes from the brisk night air
Inside a glow...
A confused man
Flexes his hand
Stares at the form
Remembering its strength

November
Bordering the edge of season sanity
One vivid and alive
The other intensifies
the sighs & the creaking
of home and man
And the comfort that is lost...

—mg

This is what I can no longer do...

I can no longer look at men's watches
as I was in the Swiss watchmaker just now
in Cambridge
having my Movado finally fixed after losing it
for the entire time we lived in Barrington
A gift from you
when we were first married
What does that mean?
Time is important to me now?
Barrington was never meant to be?
(we know that by now)
I can no longer window shop in a men's department store
as I bought most of your clothes
the wild ties with Hershey kisses and hearts
the orange sunglassed suns your patients always loved
The insane sales on men's jackets in Macy's
...buying your eggplant Joseph Abboud
I now avoid passing through to get to the other side
Like a bad joke
I can no longer go into our favorite restaurants
Yours were Chez Pascal & Parkside
22 Bowen when it was the Chart House
Always on January 6th Your birthday
Always a cold night
Maybe just a few tables Maybe snowy
Always cold
We'd get a sitter for the night
And share a bottle of wine
Except for the time they asked
if we'd like to try a glass of their feature
Opus One
It was ten dollars a glass
and just so special we said we'd have another
Back in the day when a forty dollar bar bill plus dinner
was a great expense

(as it is now)
But what the hell it was your birthday
we had twins at home and a growing practice

I can no longer listen to
Time to Say Goodbye or Orpheus
Or see the Phantom
Or watch Casablanca without you
You would say go ahead and watch Julia
You never understood this
I can see you watching 27 Dresses with the girls and all
of you crying
I never understood this
I can no longer
go by the hospital and his office without throwing the
finger
to someone I never met someone who took you from me
way too soon
I see you beside me shaking your head
you always hated my profanities
just like my mother
You made me better
I can no longer listen to Perfect Day
a metaphor of my life with you
'You made me forget myself
I thought I was
Someone else, someone good'
I can no longer sleep
Unless I play MSNBC on my computer
all night
I look for you
Most times I feel you
But I can no longer dream of you
I can no longer get in the car without
holding the medal you wore around your neck June gave
to you
as you lay in the hospital bed

Your smiling happy handsome self
trying to breathe with tubes everywhere
Our Lady of Knock
And you
Asking to help me make it through one more day For the girls
Always the girls
For us
There will always be us
And Paris
Not enough time
Time to Say Goodbye
That we first heard in Italy
Epcot Italy
Such a beautiful song
Or listen to Pachelbel
Andrea said was such a boring cello piece
And we'd laugh
Or Trois Gymnopodies
Like the time we walked in Paris
by the Erik Satie Institute
just meandering that day
Or when we rearranged our season tickets for the ballet
just to see Trois Gymnopodies
Missing L'Opera and Nureyev
because we showed up on Lundi
as the janitor sadly said Dimanche, Dimanche
and we could not speak as we walked aimlessly
around the streets of Paris
and fell into the boutique section
so perfectly dressed they courted us
with wine and couture
I can no longer play the Phantom
and not think about how we'd sing every morning
to the girls as we fed them as toddlers
all of us mesmerized by
Christine's voice
wanting her to be with the Phantom

They knew every word of it by the time they were five
I no longer look forward to October
when we were married in Mykonos
by the mayor who came one hour late
dressed in jeans and only speaking Greek
And you would not let us open the champagne
as we asked the workmen to open the shutters
that were closed for twenty years
so we could all gaze onto the harbor
The mayor's assistant so happy to have light
to view the beautiful blue Aegean
the boats and fishermen
locals shopping and the mascot pelicans
Petros and Irini
while we waited above ready to be married
Our vows in Greek said we'd educate our children
So perfect a start
Such a Perfect Day

I can no longer remember
that day you asked what was happening you could no longer
hear me you could no longer speak to me
so I took the pad and I wrote to you
I will never forget your look
you thought I'd given up
I was taking you home
Our words were meaningless
without sound without voice
you thought I gave up
I never gave up on you babe
I never gave up on us
I no longer have you
to say this to
Only my Movado
keeping perfect time

                      —mg

Part II
Leap

healer

sometimes she lapses
into flamboyancy
into hilarity
and I am entertained
beyond belief
like two old friends
having dinner

only this isn't dinner
as I choke
on my new life
of poverty
well only
financially
speaking of course

but in which
I can pluck a line or two
of self
satisfaction
of richness
and feel wealthy
beyond belief

the aging poet
who has tasted
too much of the sweet life
to be
free
    falling
        now

but suddenly
this poet's soul
has come
roaring back
so that I see
and understand

how she
helps me
get unstuck
and find
my spirit
again

my intention

she is unique
a star who fell
to guide us
with authenticity
maybe not always
subtlety
but she's real
and real
is not always part
of therapy
as I used to think

for those
whose voice
was numb
whose truth
was gone
maybe the last hope
for the hopeless
who felt they lost
this one

well to be that person
who helps
find this again
who makes
people feel better
about
themselves
is truly a gift
a work of art
and a healer
who heals broken hearts
    —mg

bicker

we argue when we're together
twenty something sixty six
estrogen city in covid zones
male influence has gone amiss
left us with unresolved
lives open wounds
finding our way out of this
but it always turns into
bicker bicker blah blah this

I can't fix you Lovely there's nothing I can fix
I can't be anymore than I can carry
and I've carried this all the way to analysis
but all I know is I'm tired
and we cannot keep doing this
worn out by three years and
a thousand night terrors
frayed nerves is our diagnosis
bicker bicker blah blah this

listen to the craziness
bicker bicker blah blah this

what is it we want of each other
balance sheet expenses
deep stabbing pain
wall of defenses
sad eyes from pure exhaustion
knowing we'll never be the same
but we can't be pugnacious
crawling our way back to sane
lifting our beaten souls from this
bicker bicker blah blah this

listen to the craziness
bicker bicker blah blah this

       —mg

**circadian
clock**

the rhythm of the soul
left me long ago
right after you took leave
and my lonely eyes did grieve
over another reality show
no cha cha left or rumba
no cheek to cheek I'm kissing
the beat of you is missing
and my lack of sleep
is what's keeping
me company
my newfound religion
that has me seeking
my circadian rhythm
I cannot find it
not even melatonin
helps this tired mind
I gave up on cbd
and those wonderful red wines
walking six and biking nine
gin and tonic sunsets
with a friend who just stopped by
Lord there's just no end
to seeking
again and again
when you've lost
the rhythm of your soul
the part of you
that searches
for itself
and you now try to start
that damn circadian clock
that just .. stopped
and the sounds of the night
echo
tick tock
tick tock
    —mg

Bookends

Isn't it rather late?
If I don't do it now
when?
I need to find my space
to walk between the rain

Time stays in these moments
flashes through my days now
When I think of what I was

When I lost you
and everything around us
our house
our work
our social connections
not very social anyway
When I lost me

And I could not look
but only squint
into the morning sun
It was then
I became the lucky one
I have bookends who hold me up
who walk me down
to the water
and back again

who pull me back
when I'm stepping off

These bookends carried me
through silent days
and sleepless nights
Through swollen corneas
rejecting contact lenses
cutting off
peripheral vision
Maybe it's better this way
to not see too clearly

Enter my bookends
who erect my bent spirit
They are not so tall
as they are statuesque
They are not so sturdy
as they are graceful
They are not so chiseled
as they exude true beauty
And carry me
when I can't walk
And discipline me
when I won't try

They do not stay
but are around

I lost my one true love
I was dead for awhile
But my bookends revived me
with lavender
with song
with photographs
Made me a home
and I accepted

Where once I gave
now I accept
It's either that or fade away
I'm not ready to fade away

Now see what they've done?
I want to memorize everything!
Look at every tree, every leaf
take a petal from November's rose
feel the icy ocean breeze on my face
Capture every sunrise
Let the others sleep
I was asleep too long

—mg

tiptoe
ever so gently
around your kindness
in case it should one day
break loose
leaving me stuck again
on an ice sheet
awash and isolated
facing a cold blue horizon
just me and my thoughts
overactive
imagination
from the ocean depth
of fear
environmental
breakdown
that I dare not
return to
now that I've been
rescued
     —mg

egret haiku

Long white birds gliding
like two Concordes to Paris
me without passport

                        I try to explain
                        their beauty as they pass by
                        But I am speechless
                                      —mg

Egret

Windswept wings of white
Waving shadows over my sight
Lost for the name of this bird
Graceful one flying forward
Not a swan or heron's secret
Early morning one call you an egret

I'm not trying to take away your peace
As you fly to the other side of the street
By the winding creek near Third Beach
This game we play when I'm within reach
I just want to share my thoughts with you
I am dazzled by your beauty egret

A nobility about you draws me near
Beauty of you brings me here
Charmed by this white ocean bird
Whose presence brings me peace
A karmic sense we are synchronistic
Mysterious one I'll call you an egret

—mg

Comeback

I could freeze here for awhile
not sure when I'd be found
some would say she lost herself
some will say she lost her mind

I won't give them the satisfaction
to see me sure as dead and gone
When did I lose myself in you
to stop being an independent one

I know how to pull myself up
Put my foot in front of the other one
Head held high I do not apologize
as I check myself and try to carry on

I'll confess to you who gave me everything
our lives became too intertwined
yes we seemed the perfect couple
a little more of yours much less mine

It was sure fun but along the way
I was swept up and I came undone
Can't believe it happened to me this woman
who believed she was an independent one

Someone who always saw herself
someone who swore to herself
she would never be like anyone else
As I try to make the comeback of my life
the independent one
⠀⠀⠀⠀⠀⠀⠀⠀⠀⠀⠀⠀⠀⠀⠀⠀—mg

For me,
Healing was the moment
When my light took my darkness
Held her close
And told her that she loved her
The unity made me whole
—ak

Today I felt like shining
How good it feels to open up
And let in my own light
                —ak

March Winds

March Winds
How they roared in!
Came late at night
such gale delight they did blow
thought they'd break through the front window
Part of it dangerous
Part of it beautiful
March Winds
Howled in
to announce their presence
no timidity for the Tempest
Gave our Pisces twins
their birthday wish!
and for me to behold this
That which changed our lives
twenty-eight years ago
That which drives us together
on another level
You may not be with us
this we know
You are always in us
we who share
always aware
of our connected souls
     —mg

fifty years

fifty year friendship
still going strong
midnight texting three ways
reminds me of the days
we would pass notes
to each other in high school
time flew
and we became
someone we didn't recognize
someone more or less the same
with responsibilities
with life's losses
and an aging face all staring
back at me
in my morning mirror
that still talks back to me
not like the sweet sixteen
who used to be so carefree
thinking about boys and cars
and sneaking out
to get high as we
walked around all over town
planning and dreaming our lives
did it work out the way
we had envisioned it?
did we get away with some of it?
because plans get changed
lives get rearranged
and the essence of who we are
still remains
the prose we wrote
the mirrors who spoke
back to us still say the same
things to us
just different refrains
as we remain
three friends who lasted fifty years
i guess there's not much i
would change
having friends who
over decades
still pass notes

—mg

Cardinal calls winter

Cardinal calls
winter morning
I lift the shade
to see the full moon
All I had to do
he sings
was to look up

—mg

egret haiku prayer

two egrets in flight
like some majestic angels
answer my prayer
                   —mg

warrior

God help the person
Who tries to conquer your quaking soul
Always somewhere between splitting the ground
halfway to hell
And raising us all up towards heaven
It's a good thing you believe you are your own god
We need your fury for human matters
—ak

high

I've seen the highs and lows of life
So high you thought you thought you were riding the waves
at Waikiki
So low you found yourself on the sole of someone's worn out Wellie
And you take these with you
Always
in that clutch of yours
and you snap it shut
Such sensitivity!
You've had your ups and downs
like when you were the elevator
operator
And now you're somewhere else staring at the buttons
You've got to push something
as you are stuck
between Purgatory and Waikiki
On your way to Paradise my dears
I can feel it this time
Just take out the smudged 4x6 one more time
Kiss it lovingly while holding onto Knock
Borrow a board
Ride the risk
Then call it out to the universe
Go on
You can do it and no one's looking
Call it out call it
So loud you will break the sound
barrier!
                              —mg

white and weathered

she's white and weathered
she used to be young in leather
now her cadence is tethered
to a 5 mile radius of old style capes
and windy New England weather
waiting for a nice spring day
to ride his Specialized Roubaix
feeling what the heart can only free
trying to do the first ten in forty
no time to stop for the birds this morning
like she's training for the Tour de France
riding those wooing hills in the distance
gliding along the ocean breeze
shaking off whatever is left of the lonely
woman who's wiser than weathered
wearing the smile of young and free
momentarily

—mg

As if..
For Kim & Victoria

As if I could take what we had
our thirty year engagement
delicately wrap it in
Tiffany mosaic tissue paper
place it in a velvet jeweled box
keep it safely tucked away
to take it's place among the discarded
and forgotten

As if I don't feel you always
in the missing and the meaning
measured in these years by
what I wear in thought in being
maybe more than this
below my skin your pulse
that beats with my own beating
that speaks your name in sleep
and deceives my eyes
with what they're seeing

As if you are not still with us
in our son's and daughters' eyes
in their sound and sentence
in what they say
their wit their mother's eloquence
the fabric of family
the fine threads spun and woven
you will not find a stitch so perfect
that forms our own pattern
spun like pure silk lightness
or sturdy tweed tightness
the beauty that we designed
worn the rest of our lives

because who's to say this
is all there is for any of us?

As if we can just push all of this aside
to make new memories when
we have these intrinsic ones
wrapped in such luxury
that calls to memory
something grand something beyond
what we know because
in its essence
life is not just the here and now
but the interlacing fibre of
permanence

—mg

Three Julys

What's the first most important word I thought?
It's love
one could argue this but I'd rather not
Then.. What's the second most important word?
It's home
home is everything to anyone
to the smallest of beings and to those
who are human beings
all of us
search for home
and love

There came a time I had to leave
in July
Three Julys to be exact
and I said to myself
No, this can't be
This will not keep happening to me
And I rose somehow out of despair
Oh yes, I had help all around
They seemed to come from everywhere
And when Julys no longer carry this meaning
for me
Maybe I'll return the favor for
it was my love who said to me
Take me home hon
This is what I gave to you
And this is what we created
for our family
Because home is everything
And home comes from love
Or does love come from home?
the order does not matter
both he gave to me

      —mg

You are never going to be ready
One day it's just going to happen
You will look at each other while lying in bed
The place will remain the same
  but you have changed
Like going to an old street where you grew up
Revisiting a childhood memory
Now, older
You recognize the familiarity
With deadened feelings
Some kind of sadness
That everything blends into memory
And you still won't be ready
The truth is you will never be ready
To bury what is dead
                      —ak

Chiron
myth or man
unlikely hero
born to rejection
strength and grace
of a colt
who became
a stallion

Saved by the
sun god
Apollo
who gave him words of poetry
to heal
his warrior wounds
and wisdom
to become
a teacher

Chiron
Wounded healer
take me back to Greece
to Mykonos
where memories exist
part real part myth

Apollo
whose warmth
kisses our
self sabotaged faces
restores us
from what
love's loss
erases

Like the Centaurus
a shower of stars
above us
falling
giving guidance
another try

To those of us
who wish on shooting stars
who seek to be better
than what we are

Yes more than any other
I understand you
Chiron
When I look up to
the constellations
When I converse
with nature
am I only part human?
You who
outline the southern skies
Illuminate this poet's eyes
restore beauty inside
because I'm not feeling it
and I've stopped
wondering why

We make our myths
part real part dream
Nature and human
Instinct and reasoning
Reclaiming justice
without
and within

We find ourselves in parts
searching
to be whole again
Help lift our eyes
toward the mythological sky
Be our spiritual guide
ruled by the planets
Our Wounded Healer
Chiron

                —mg

Somewhere in the spring of my life

Somewhere
In the spring of my life
A seed was implanted deep into my brain
And it bloomed, it bloomed
There are no words that can wrap themselves around what it has now become
Its petals burst
With everything I have ever known
Its dizzy pleasures
Ache with recognition
And chant
I am, I am
Love
So,
If I have nothing else to show
When this world ravages our age, our kin, our homes, and our dreams
Just remember that I held that flower in my hand
And that was enough for me

—ak

Page 86: Captiva, May 1st 2016
—mg

www.ingramcontent.com/pod-product-compliance
Lightning Source LLC
Chambersburg PA
CBHW051457290426
44109CB00016B/1790